Avoiding Relapse

Avoiding Relapse

Catching Your Inner Con

Lynne Namka

Authors Choice Press

San Jose New York Lincoln Shanghai

Avoiding Relapse
Catching Your Inner Con

Authors Choice Press
an imprint of iUniverse.com, Inc.

For information address:
iUniverse.com, Inc.
5220 S 16th, Ste. 200
Lincoln, NE 68512
www.iuniverse.com

ISBN: 0-595-19613-6

Printed in the United States of America

Contents

APPENDICES

Acknowledgements

As the understanding in the field of addictions grows, we have a wealth of dedicated clinicians and researchers who add to our body of knowledge of assisting people in their challenge to stay clean and sober. Thanks go to the following people for their ideas in compiling this book.

Bill W. for starting the whole recovery movement.
Carl Jung, who wrote Bill W., telling him that spirituality is a necessary part of recovery.
Terry Gorski for his tremendous contribution to the field of relapse prevention.
Stephanie Brown for her developmental model of addictions.
Rick Glantz for his intervention model for dealing with constant cravings.
Patrick Carnes for his books on sexual addictions and Internet addictions.
Ken Moses for his model of the layers of denial.
William Glasser on his concept of positive and negative addictions.
Martin Seligman for his research and work of learned helplessness and optimism.
Virginia Satir for her groundbreaking ideas of congruence and straight communication.
G. D. Walters for describing cutoffs.
Stanislav and Christine Grof, Jacqueline Small and Tav Sparks for their idea of addictions as a search for Spirit.

Roger Callahan for Thought Field Therapy, which helps release anxiety associated with craving.

James Prochaska, John Norcross and Carlo DiClemente on the process of how people change.

And the researchers at the American Psychological Association 1998 symposium of Cravings and Cognition.

Thanks also go to friends Pat Malloy, Rebecca Hatchett and Jerry Snyder who have contributed ideas to this book. Finally thanks to Mary Dillon for making editing suggestions and Gordon Harnack for the book cover, and Gordon, Mary Fredona and Phyllis Fredona for editing assistance.

Introduction

A desperate woman called me in the middle of the night. She couldn't get through to her Narcotics Anonymous sponsor. She had tried to reach her pusher to sell her the drug of choice, which was Speed. Fortunately for her, the pusher was not at home. She was frantically dialing numbers of psychologists and she got me. She told me that she had been clean and sober from drugs for seven months with the help of Narcotics Anonymous. But today, she had gotten a diagnosis of HIV and cervical cancer. Life had become too much for her to bear and she needed a fix.

We hit it off and talked for an hour on the phone about recovery. I teased her about her Inner Con who had been crazy to do Speed again after all her hard work of getting her life under control and regaining custody of her children. She laughed and said she was okay for the time being. I gave her some options about what she could do rather than call her pusher. Then she paid me a compliment about my approach. "Are you an addict," she asked? "You know what you are talking about. You think like an addict."

Now, I'm fortunate in that I don't have destructive addictive behavior. My pattern is co-dependency, which I've written about in my book, *The Doormat Syndrome*. But I do understand the addictive process and the erroneous thinking, which goes with it. My background includes training with Virginia Satir and Cognitive-Behavioral, Transpersonal and

Buddhist Psychology. From there I branched into the study of addictions. I counsel addicts and their families in my private psychology practice.

I lay awake long after that phone call thinking of the suffering that addicts and their families go through. I thought of the pain of a four-year-old boy who deeply loves his father who is hooked on cocaine and the dad's unfulfilled promises. I remembered the teenage gang girls I sent to inpatient recovery programs who continued to struggle with their alcohol and drug use. I recalled the twelve-year-olds who are flirting with pot because they believe that it will reduce the stress they were feeling. I thought of the pain that addictions had caused my own family. And the man who has a genius IQ, who is diabetic and is destroying himself with alcohol while justifying his choices.

I recalled the rationalizations and justifications that I had heard people make over the years about their choices to get high. Then I looked at the excuses that I had made to myself about doing things that were not in my own best interests. At that moment I realized that we all have an Inner Con.

That night, I made the decision to write this book on relapse prevention, tying together information drawn from the addiction field, the cognitive behavior approach and spirituality.

Addictions are a major problem of our times with the huge numbers of our population who are escaping from everyday reality. Eleven million Americans abuse alcohol. One million people are regular heroin users and 700,000 use cocaine regularly. Countless other millions are struggling with various other drugs, eating disorders, gambling, shopping, Internet addictions and sex or relationship addictions.

There is help available. At this time in history, there is more information available to assist people who want more than a life filled with addiction. Millions of people are in 12-step programs and/or have gone through recovery programs and are fighting to remain clean and sober. For some, it is a very tough fight.

This book is written for people who have some sophistication about addictions and are looking for ways to make the process of recovery easier. People who are prone to addictions need all they help they can get in staying sober. *Avoiding Relapse: Catching Your Inner Con* will help you identify and break into your negative mind games.

How to Use This Book

> "In your hands will be placed the exact results of your thoughts; you will receive that which you earn, no more, no less. Whatever your present environment may be, you will fall, remain, or rise with your thoughts, your wisdom, desire, as great as your dominant aspirations."
> *James Allen, As a Man Thinketh*

Happiness starts from the inside out. How you commune with yourself is reflected in the world. We are our thoughts. Thoughts are us! Our thoughts and words make up who we are. What we think and say is what we draw to us. Like energy attracts like energy. The Law of Attraction reminds us that we draw matter and energy to us that is of a like vibration. As the poet Richard Gilder said, "Sow thou sorrow and thou shall reap it. Sow thou joy and thou shall keep it."

So mark up this book! Personalize it. Make it your own manual for staying sober. Write your own ideas in it. Underline or highlight the areas that are meaningful to you. Turn down the corners of pages you want to go back to. There is plenty of white space on the pages for you to add your own observations about what you think and say that might send you down the destructive road. The concepts presented here are big and the words sparse, so you can add your own thoughts and ideas of keeping you clean and sober.

Read the book over and over to break into your own negative ways of thinking. Challenge negativity until it no longer holds an emotional charge for you. Read parts of the book out loud to yourself, hearing the power of your own voice. Pick the book up often when you have a few minutes of time and open it and see what pages you choose. See what conclusions you come to.

Identify with positive ideas on the pages that empower you. Hang out with the concepts that connect you with your Higher Power. Sit with your Truth. It will set you free.

1

CONGRATULATIONS—YOU HAVE MADE THE SOBRIETY PRIORITY

Congratulations! You've Become Clean and Sober

You've become clean and sober. It has taken a lot of hard work to get you here. You've finally gotten yourself free from a life controlled by addiction. You've made the sobriety priority. Life has taken a rosy turn since you decided to get your life back under your own management. Pat yourself on the back for your hard work and accomplishment. What a deal you've worked out for yourself!

Now let's get practical. Let's get real. Living a life of sobriety in a society that encourages addictions is a challenge. Make no mistake about it, addictive habits die hard. The desire to use has many big hooks that can undermine you. Your negative mind set that caused your life to go out of control chasing addictions is very crafty.

Creating Your Mental Health Tool Kit

Addictions come in all kinds of flavors and sizes. Some addictions are mind-blowing. Some are life stealing. Out-of-control addictions always involve loss. They create family and relationship problems, health issues, job jeopardy or failure in some aspect of your life. Sometimes the desire to go back to your former destructive way of life sneaks up on you without your even being aware that you are getting caught. You need all the ammunition you can get to live a life of sobriety.

Everyone who goes through the trouble of becoming clean and sober also needs a tool kit of techniques and strategies to get you through tough times. You can add some strong mental health tools for your tool-box of relapse prevention. Positive mind tools assist you in keeping your thoughts straight, so you will stay straight, no matter what. Your mind has to become completely clean and sober before your life does. You can learn the useful tools to keep all those important sobriety goals you have achieved and gain courage, hope, honesty and perseverance.

The Con Is That Part of Your Mind Who Hooks You Back into Self-Sabotaging Behavior

Relapse into your old addictive habits can be a possibility at any time. The danger of relapse is that you will slip back into former unhealthy patterns that created havoc in your life. Addictions are always about loss—the loss of your identity.

Deep within the recesses of your mind, lies the Con! Your Inner Con specializes in seduction. It attempts to manipulate you by focusing on fear and anxiety.

The Con is that part of your mind that tries to hook you back into your old way of rationalizing that alcohol and drugs can be a part of your life. It is exacting, greedy and never satisfied. It is a hard taskmaster, always wanting more, more, more of whatever got you in trouble in the first place. It will say anything to get you to use. The Con is the Big Lie!

Learning to hear and interrupt your nagging Inner Con is a major tool in your toolbox of relapse prevention.

What's The Quality of Your Thoughts?

Heavy use of addictive substances can mess with your thinking. Continual alcohol or drug use can result in brain chemistry changes, which play havoc with your thinking. You may have severe errors in thinking about what is in your best interests.

Heavy use of alcohol or drugs can change the way you view yourself. Addictions can subtly change your values and even affect what you deem right and wrong. Your self-esteem can change in a negative direction without your even being aware of it. The siren call of addiction can lead you to believe that using is better than not using, even though there are dire consequences. Your dependence on addictions may have even eroded your meaning and purpose in life.

Preventing relapse begins with your getting clear on what type of life is worth living. Getting back your good self-esteem that sobriety brings can become the top priority in your life. Emotional well-being is your being satisfied with who you are. Pride in yourself as a human being is part of finding contentment and happiness in your life.

Negative Moods Often Precede Relapse

Do you remember how rotten you feel when you are down? Now there is research that shows negative emotions can trigger relapse! Cravings haunt you more when discomfort, anxiety and depression set in. And every single person in the world has to deal with negative moods. Most addicts have never learned to deal with their emotional and physical discomforts. Instead they turned to their drug of choice to self medicate the miseries of life.

The choice to reach for the bottle or the drug again can be a stress driven choice. New research shows that addicts suffer feelings of stress in their body as the previous fix wears off. The addiction actually creates more stress for you just before you go back at it again! This physical discomfort combined with feeling down beguiles you into using again to calm yourself.

How to Throw Yourself Back into Addictive Behavior

Here is a typical scenario when you are feeling bad. You start to feel overwhelmed and under loved. You start to think of going for your addiction to avoid feeling uncomfortable, nervous, inhibited or bored. Body tension sets in. Obsessive thoughts and impulsive behavior can drive you to drug-seeking behavior if you give into them. If you are not aware of the addictive thinking aspects of addiction, you could easily become snared back in.

So take a good hard look at your life. Look at both during and after your bouts with the destructive addictions.

- Do you do things that increase your feeling good about yourself?
- What do you do to self soothe and take down tension?
- How do you take yourself out of the blues?
- What do you do when you feel sorry for yourself?
- What do you use to calm yourself down?

Strong Cravings and Addictive Preoccupations Can Tempt You to Relapse

When you first refrain from your addiction, anxiety can loom up big time. The nervous feelings that come up when you aren't using are big-time withdrawal. Physiological withdrawal lasts only until the drug clears the body. Then you are left with the underhanded thinking that you must use to relax.

Cravings begin when you are not satisfied with how you are feeling. Then the "wantas" cravings start in. The negative talk in your mind begins to do a number on you. This is the Con talking, big time! The fabrication that can accompany craving is that there is a magic pill, drink, substance or activity that will make bad feelings go away. The irrational belief is "I must get rid of these bad feelings no matter what the cost." The error in thinking here is that it is not okay to feel bad. Everyone has bad feelings at times. It is what we do with the feelings that count.

Identify your cravings chatter and break into it before it gets a strong hold on you. Full-blown cravings that run amuck can send you over into the "gottas." The "gottas" are when you convince yourself that you have to go for that drug of choice. The danger point is when the "wantas" start to feel out of control and move you over into the "gottas."

Break into that chain of lies, beliefs, cravings and behavior that sends you back down that road to your worst nightmare.

After Detox, the Craving Chain Will Go Away Whether You Use Or Not!

Know this for sure—intense cravings do not equal using. Many people report high levels of cravings and refrain from going back to their addictive behavior.

You can get through this bad stage of craving by calling your distress by name. Become conscious about what is happening in your body and in your mind. Tell yourself, "This is a craving. This is just a craving. I'm feeling anxious/bored/ incomplete so I'm craving. That is all it is. I'm feeling shaky, but it will pass. Even though my heart is racing and I feel sick to my stomach, this too will pass. This is just feeling scared. I can wait it out. It is just a craving. That is all it is."

Guess what? Cravings come. Cravings go away. Feelings change. Desire passes. Obsessions decrease IF you don't give them power. It is what you do with cravings that count. Dwell on them or plan to act on them and they continue. Use the handy tools from your mental health tool kit on them and they will pass.

The average craving lasts fifteen to twenty minutes. Get past this time frame and you have it made! Do whatever it takes to outlast them. Distract yourself from them. Out shout them. Outwait them. Outwit them. Scream at them. Call a friend for help if you need it to make it through the bad time. Cravings may come back later, but they will go away again if you don't dwell on them. Your sense of self is stronger than your cravings.

Deciding to go back to your drug of choice is a chain of behaviors that gets stronger if you give power to any link of it. Break the chain. Break into the cravings chain at its earliest weak link. Remind yourself, "Cravings come and go. The desire will shift if you don't give in to it. This too will pass. I can choose healthy self-soothing activities to release these empty, bored or anxious feelings."

What Part of You Is Invested in Your Addiction? Your Inner Con!

Your Inner Con is that scheming, conniving part of your mind that tempts you to go back to your addiction! Your Inner Con is a master of lies to persuade you to use your substance or activity of choice. It is a fear-based part of you, *but it is not who you are.* That treacherous Con is a dominant ego part, which acts out of negativity and fear. It clings to the attachment of limitation and restriction of self-growth. Its embittered voice leads you to your gateway to excess. Its constant nitpicking erodes your sense-of-self.

This inflated fragment of the ego is a subpart of your total personality. Your Inner Con is absorbed in totally protecting and preserving itself. It feeds your fixation and agonizes about not being complete without using. It seduces, swindles and victimizes you to go against yourself and your better nature.

The Con's job is to confuse you with what is right and wrong for your life. It divides your psyche and creates mistrust in yourself. Its purpose is to keep hounding you until you weaken and give in.

What Makes Up Your Inner Con?

The Con is a group of fear-based characters whose only purpose is to keep hounding until you weaken and give in to going back to those self-destructive addictive behaviors. These parts of you clamor and raise a ruckus trying to force you back to using.

When you are in the clutches of cravings, ask yourself:

- What part of me makes me feel overwhelmed?
- What part of me sends me into irrational destructive thinking?
- What part of me steals my personal power?
- What part tells me to drink, drug or choose some unhealthy activity?
- What part wields the big hook to pull me back in?
- What parts of me fuels my addictions?

The Con is your worst enemy who acts like your best buddy to get you to use.

The Con is not who you are.

2

YOUR CAST OF FEAR-BASED PARTS

Your Fear-Based Parts Who Make Up The Con:

Your Inner Pusher Who Pushes You to Exhaustion, Then Pushes You to Use

The Pusher is your workaholic part that compensates fatigue by using. The Pusher part rationalizes, "I've worked hard so I can…I've been putting in so many hours of overtime, I need to relax by…It's Friday night and this has been a long, hard week. I deserve to…I'm not having fun anymore living sober, so I'll…."

Your Inner Victim Who Feels Sorry for Yourself Because You Can't Use

Your Inner Victim is a sniveler who argues that nothing ever works for it. It whines. It snivels. The Victim part says things like, "Sobriety is miserable. I never get to party anymore. It's not fair. Why can't I drink like everyone else? If I can't use, I don't want to do anything. I avoid new interests and hobbies. I can't cope. I've just got to use to deal with my rotten life. Nothing ever works for me. Poor me, I can never get high again."

If you give into the Victim part, you will always feel deprived and left out. Victim dwells on things you can't have anymore. It moans "I'm lost without my drug of choice. It's awful I can't have it. I can't stand not having it. I'm losing my friends. I'm no fun to be with when I'm sober. Life isn't worth living if I can't have my fun. I'll die without it."

Your Helpless Sucker Who Says That You Are Hooked Forever

Your Helpless Sucker creates a sense of powerlessness that is pervasive regarding addictions. It says, "This addiction is stronger than I am. I have no will power when it comes to…There is nothing I can do about this. Poor me, there is nothing else left for me but to…I will always have these feelings of being hooked."

The Part Who Believes Conflict Is Bad so Uses to Avoid Angry Thoughts

This Avoidance part has been taught that anger and confrontation are wrong. It uses addictive substances to numb out the anger. This part denies that anger is a normal part of being a human being. The avoidance of anger parts says, "I can't be angry. I feel hurt about our fight so I can use…To calm me down, I'll do some…I can't stand being frustrated, so I'll mellow out by…."

Your Inner Narcissist Who Feels Entitled to Use

The constant theme of being overly self-involved is "I owe me a good time." This part boasts, "I deserve to use to feel good. I'm entitled to go out and have a few laughs. Well I've been good, that it's okay for me to do a little. I can handle it. I ought to be able to go out and party."

Your Inner Narcissist searches for whatever reason it can find to fill up that empty place inside with addictive behavior. Anytime you hear yourself saying, "I deserve to have…" check out that destructive thinking about how you are owed a break so you can use. Ask yourself "Who is doing the talking about deserving here?"

Your Feeling Hurt and Betrayed Part Who Sets You Up for Using

Any disappointment in love or friendship can become the excuse for using. The Hurt and Betrayed part says, "He dumped me, so I'll get drunk. The one I love chose another, so I'm going to…." Hurt and anger justifies your going for the addiction when you feel put out. It can't stand any miscommunication with friends or family. It moans, "They don't understand me, so I can use…." "Someone I care about is on the outs with me so I'll…." "They are mad at me, so I can do what I want. I'll show them."

The Introverted Part Who Uses Alcohol and Drugs As a Social Lubricant

This is one uptight part that uses alcohol or drugs to be more spontaneous socially. This part rationalizes, "I'm bored being by myself so I'll hit the bar. I'm awkward socially so I drink to loosen up and talk easier. I'm lonely, so I can use…I'm more comfortable with others if I take a drink or two."

The Part Who Dwells on Your Rotten Past and Predicts a Rotten Future

This Rotten Childhood part tries to convince you that you will always be as limited as your past. The Victim part cries and whines, "I had a rough childhood. My parents didn't love me, so I'm unlovable. My dad was abusive, so now I can abuse myself. My folks didn't care about me, so I don't care what happens to me. I can't change how I am because my dad was an alcoholic. It's in my genes, so I can't change how I am."

The error is thinking the chaotic past will predict the future. The assumption is that a terrible childhood should continue into a terrible adulthood that must embrace addictions. Actually it's your daily choices that keep your major soap opera going. Your present and your future are both dependent on what choices you make today, not what you did in the past.

Your Inner Impulsive Kid Who Can't Delay Gratification

Your Impulsive part can't wait and must have what it wants when it wants it! It justifies, "What the heck. I can't live with these feelings of wanting something. Let's go for it now! These obsessive thoughts are too strong. I have to go get my drug of choice right now. Pressure is building up. I can't take this. I feel compelled to use to release this agitation. Now! Now! Now!"

Your Inner Wild and Crazy Part Who Thinks Life Is Too Darn Serious

Your Wild and Crazy part can't stand to be bored. It is a party, party part that craves stimulation. It says, "Gimmee fun! Where's the excitement? I have to party to have fun. I need instant fun. My fun is to get high. I deserve exhilaration and a sense of well-being. Bring on that rush."

Your Rebellious Child Who Finds Excitement in Being Bad

Your Rebellious Child inside delights in feeling good about being bad. The Rebel thinks of the appeal of taking risks and living life on the edge. Fueled by excitement of the chase, your Rebel throws common sense and caution to the winds. The headiness of rebellion rushes you down that fast lane to excess. The Rebel acts out defiantly when others who care level with you about straightening up.

The Rebel part probably started when you were a small child who hated being controlled by outside authority. Now it has become your controller. Your Rebel hardens to keep you believing it that is better to live the lifestyle addiction. It hangs out with people who give you permission to pull back from conventional values of mainstream society. The Rebel part is a dissident who feels superior and looks down on nonusers. It says that the outside world's motivation and ideals for living a good life are stupid.

When you continue to live out the Rebel, you immerse yourself in a culture that reinforces using. Life long rebellion can be a coming-of-age issue that sticks around too long. The Rebel speaks with pride and looks down on those who live the straight life. It says, "What do they know? I'm born to be wild. What they say is stupid. It doesn't apply to me. I'm different so I can handle this. My way of doing my life is best. Using is fun. Partying is where I'm at. I will never walk the straight and narrow path even if it kills me."

Get real. If you are an adult and your life stinks due to your alcohol or drug use, you are not a Rebel. You are a stinking alcoholic or drug user!

The Part That Grabs Hold of Any Reason to Relapse

Good news or bad; it makes no difference. Any excuse to use will do here. This Grabber part looks for reasons and agrees with any rationale for starting up your addictions again.

This looking-for-any-excuse part reasons, "I lost my job, so I'll drown my sorrows. I got a promotion so let's celebrate. My evaluation at work was lousy, so bring on the…I got a terrible diagnosis of illness, so…Let's have a beer blast to show off our new house. Let's celebrate my new job by partying."

Your Creature of Habit That Uses to Get Out of Body Discomfort

Sometimes it is the discomfort of your body that sets the stage for going back to using. Catch your typical negative body state and thoughts that signal that you are obsessing over your addiction. Now that you are sober, notice how you stress your body by thinking of using and returning to that out-of-control life.

- Where do you typically hold tension in your body?
- What body sensation is upsetting to you? Your nervous stomach?
- Where do you ache? What hurts? Your tight neck? Your aching back?
- Watch your breathing pattern when you are upset. Do you hold your breath?
- Where does your body tense up to give you permission to relapse?
- What part of your body says? "I can't stand this. It's too terrible to bear."

So your body and mind team up to create those Con thoughts. Your body gets nervous and tense. Your mind tells you to go ahead and use. Warning! A tense body can be a setup for using and then disaster.

Your Master Justifier Who Looks for Others to Blame

If you are not sure whether you're blaming others for your problems, call a neutral friend to give your feedback. Virtually anything said followed by "That's just the way I am" is denial. Watch your two-part sentences that have the word "but" or "because" in them. They often contain rationalizations and justifications.

Sometimes you speak the truth in the first half of the sentence, and then state your denial in the second half. These end up being blame statements as you try to avoid responsibility for your own choices.

Be a vigilant observer of your thoughts and words so that you do not become a Master Justifier of your misdeeds. Here are some typical Master Justifier ways of thinking and talking:

> "I know I shouldn't have gone out partying, **but** I needed a
> break from work.
> I shouldn't have hit her, **but** she made me so angry.
> I'm sorry that I spent so much at the mall, **but** he spends
> much more on drinking.
> It's okay for me to have an affair, **because** my spouse continues to use.
> I didn't want to go gambling at the casino, **but** she talked me
> into it.
> I wish I hadn't eaten the whole cake, **but** I was upset because
> he called me fat."

The combination of body and mind urging you to get some relief by using sets up your Master Justifier to use words of permission-giving which are called "Cutoffs."

3

WARNING! YOUR INNER CON IS THE KING OF CUTOFFS

Cutoffs Are Big Con Lies That Cut Off Your Common Sense

Cuttoffs are things you tell yourself, saying it's okay to use. They are those seductive whoppers that you tell yourself on the rocky road to relapse.

Cutoffs are any words that help you distort reality. They are falsehoods you tell yourself to readjust what you consider to be right and wrong. They include those thoughts, words and behaviors that trick you into becoming dysfunctional again. Cutoff words are insidious rationalizations that cause you to throw your common sense out the window.

Cutoffs help you minimize in your own mind the damage you have done. They are the whoppers you tell yourself in order to ignore the severe emotional, interpersonal, and physical consequences of continuing to use. They rationalize your actions of being okay with continuing your addictive behavior.

The Ruler of Cutoffs urges you to engage in dysfunctional behavior. Your Cutoff part says, "I can handle it. It won't hurt me." "Oh, go ahead, you know you want it. One time won't matter." "I'll just take one…"

Cutoffs are rampant when you are searching for permission to go back to your former drinking and drugging behavior. Your Inner Con is a seductive dictator who uses Cutoffs to lead you back to addictions.

There Are Layers of Denial before You Are Ready to Know the Truth About Your Addiction

Some of the most challenging things in life start with the letter D. Disappointment, difficulties, danger, divorce, dismissal, destruction, disaster, depression, drugs and drinking and defenses, as in defensive thinking.

Perhaps the biggest D word of all is Denial. Cutoffs are always denial. When you are in denial, you reject the truth about what is really happening to you. Addicts move back and forth between these different layers of denial. Pulling the wool over your eyes just gives you scratchy eyes.

You know you are caught up in addictions when one or more areas of your life are disrupted by your habit. You are hooked if there is dependence on an activity or a substance that affects your relationship with your family, friends and job or creates financial or legal problems. When using becomes the constant focus in your life, permeates your thoughts and behavior, and defines who you are, you are addicted.

You can become so absorbed with your addiction that you don't realize that you've disconnected from loved ones. It's frightening to know the truth of how much your addiction has run your life. It's alarming to realize how much your habit hurts the ones you love. Resistance manifests as not knowing what is best for you.

But Hey, You Are Human. Humans Are Masters of Denial!

You have shortcomings and character defects just like everyone else. If you can't see the truth about your addictive ways of thinking, ask a trusted friend to give you a reality check. If people who care about you are telling you things about yourself that you just can't understand, then you are probably in denial. The Con works hard to keep you in denial.

When you are ready to stretch and grow, deeper understanding comes in. Honesty is the best gift you can give yourself. When you are ready to know the truth about your situation, you can set yourself free. You can learn to cut off those Cutoffs and move past the denial.

Denial of the Facts: There Is No Problem!

This denial part will not see any problem associated with addictive behavior. This part refuses to face facts. It says, "I do not have a problem. I am not addicted to…I can't know about this myself. Don't tell me about…It is not so. I don't want to hear about this. No problemo!"

Denial of the Significance of the Facts: There's a Problem, but It's Not Important!

This form of denial minimalizes the addiction. It says, "Yes, so I use, but it's no big deal. This habit doesn't affect me. I don't use that much. So what? The situation is not bad enough to warrant my making any changes. I use just a little bit. I don't do it that often."

Denial of the Duration of the Problem: This Is Just a Short-Term Problem!

This type of denial insists that the addiction is temporary. It tries to buy time to continue the bad habits by insisting, "Yes I've got a problem but it won't last much longer. Next week I'll stop using…This is only a temporary stage. It isn't going to last. I'll wait it out. I'll stop tomorrow. Next week it will be different. I'll get better soon on my own. It will go away."

Denial of Emotions of the Importance of the Facts: I'm Numbed Out and Can't Change!

This is the part that feels emotionally paralyzed and focuses on helplessness. This type of denial digs a hole and jumps right in, instead of going directly to problem solving. This part convinces you to believe that you don't have the inner resources to promote change. It whines, "Yes, I know it is important, but I'm immobilized. It's too much. I can't deal with this. It is hopeless. It's no use trying to be different. I can't change who I am. I am helpless in changing how I feel."

Denial Regarding Public Exposure: I Can't Go Back to Self-Help Meetings!

This denial part is so ashamed, embarrassed and fearful of being found out. It hangs its head and hides, saying, "I can't let anyone know. I can't go back to meetings. My shame is too great. I can't admit this relapse to anyone else. I'm so embarrassed and just can't go public with this."

Denial Due to Omnipotent Beliefs: I Am God and Am in Control of Everything!

Pride is the culprit at work here. This grandiose part says, "I can work it out myself. I'll try harder and the problem will go away. I can change on my own. I don't need any help with this. I can stop using whenever I want to. Don't tell me what to do! Let me do this all by myself."

Denial That Fosters False Hope for Future Use: My Drug of Choice Is Still an Option!

This denial part hangs on to the secret hope that you can use someday. It never truly gives up the addictive thinking. It sees sobriety as a temporary condition. It is caught in the false hope that you can go back to the addictive behavior. This denial rationalizes, "It will work for me in the future. I'm different now. I can use now that I've been away from it. I can handle it now. I'll just take one drink or hit. I refuse to give up my fantasies of using someday."

Denial of Family Secrets: Keep Bad Things Secret No Matter What!

This part is loyal to the family where people are hurting each other. It agrees to hiding things, saying, "I must act as if nothing bad has happened. I must push the bad things under the rug like we have always done. I can't share these regrets, fears or worries with my family members. I have to keep a stiff upper lip and shove the bad feelings down. I must stay in dysfunctional relationships that would be better off dissolved."

Denial of Lifestyle Hazards: I can Hang out at Bars and Parties and Stay Clean!

People, places and things that encourage using can set you up for relapse. Environmental influences can affect how we act. We come under stimulus control of triggers that set the stage for returning to bad habits. This is the denial part of you that looks for happiness in all the wrong places.

The social setups for using are peer pressure and seeing addictive behavior as normal and desirable. "But everybody does…" is the cutoff that justifies using. Cues in the environment associated with addictive behavior shout at you "Go for it." The danger zones are bars, parties, celebrations, holidays and vacations where alcohol and drugs are prevalent.

Cue-induced craving happens when you drive by your favorite bar, smell cigarette smoke or go to a party where people are using and you want to use. A common visual cue such as talking on the phone can trigger the association with reaching for a cigarette. Or watching a ball game with your buddies throws you back into your craving for a beer. Cues that are associated with using reactivate those memory centers in the brain and set up a strong desire to use. What you see or what you smell can become what you want!

Denial That Your Friends Can Tempt You Into Using!

People who encourage you to join them in using are not true friends when you are working for sobriety. Friendships that are organized around getting high are not real friendships. The focus is on getting the desired substance or activity—not on intimacy and connection with others. These so-called friends are rarely there for you when you try to leave the using scene. A true friend is someone who is there when you are down and wants the best for you.

Drop those friends that enable you to use again. And you are not being a friend to yourself if you enable yourself in habits that are not in your best interests.

Catch the thoughts that tempt you to go to familiar places where you habitually used. Arrest those thoughts that say "Go ahead, Dude, come on out to the bar. You can handle it." Avoid addictive triggers of those people and places that create in you the desire to use. Stay away from places where addictive use is the norm, where you start thinking it's okay to use. Avoid that "near occasion of sin" that does you in!

Denial of Responsibility: Oh Sure I Use, But It's Not My Fault!

Sometimes it hurts so bad that it's hard to see your part of the problem. Somebody has to be bad, and it sure can't be you. So you look outside yourself to find someone else to blame. You don't want to own the bad feelings so throw them on someone else. This thin-skinned part takes things personally. It can't stand being criticized. Then it looks around to see if it can throw the bad feelings onto others. But there are costs. By blaming others, you lose your opportunity to grow.

Reproaching others when you feel bad may bring about a flash of feeling better. But increased self-esteem at the expense of ignoring how you create your own misery is transient. Believing it is not your fault is an insidious Con trick to let yourself off the hook.

Blaming others is lying to oneself to make your dysfunctional behavior seem acceptable. Anytime you blame anyone outside yourself for what's wrong with you is denial, big time! Anytime you say, "He/she/they are wrong and they have to fix it," you're not owning your part of the problem. This is your Master Justifier trying to con you. Rationalizing one's behavior maintains the denial of it's okay to use.

Denial of Shame Based Feelings: I Can't Let Myself Know How Bad I Feel Inside!

Shame is a fear-based internal state accompanied by feelings of being unworthy and unlovable. These deep-seated feelings conjure up brief, intense, painful feelings of mortification due to being seen as inadequate. Feelings of shame keep us caught in fear of being found out by others. The perceived deficit is so humiliating that the person goes to any lengths to hide the flawed self.

The causes of shame that have been put upon us by others include betrayal and broken trust. Harsh, critical parental behavior produces shame-prone children. A parent's high expectations of behavior and disapproval for failure create shame. Parental withdrawal, rejection or favoritism of a sibling causes deep fears of abandonment. Parental humiliation and punishment for failure, distress, or crying, creates the need to hide vulnerability. The child feels that he must be really bad or his parents would love him. In addition, physical and sexual abuses imprint major feelings of being devalued and unworthy in the victim.

You can induce shame in yourself by engaging in morally inappropriate behavior. Worrying what others think, fears of public failure and social disapproval lead to fears of rejection and abandonment. Having a life out of control due to addictions can foster great shame, which then makes you want more of your addictive substance or behavior.

4

GUILT AND SHAME:
THE FUNNY TWINS

Guilt: A Voice from Your Conscience

Guilt is a feeling that we did something wrong. Guilt says, "I did something bad. I was wrong. I must pay." Violations of society's values around sexual and aggressive behavior, being different, and looked down upon by others, are common causes of guilt. Guilt comes from your conscience that says, "Clean up your act."

Guilt is about actions, shame is about the self. Guilt says, "I did a bad thing." Shame says, "I am bad." The shame core builds up with many events of guilt. Guilt added to shame lead to the global belief of "I am unworthy. I am unlovable," which must be avoided at all costs.

Shame Is the Shaper of Symptoms

Addictions always have a deep core of shame. Shame can hide underground and stay there. Repressed shame leads to substituting more acceptable emotions such as anger, depression and anxiety to reduce the internal tension. Other defenses of shame include macho behavior, intellectualization and shutting down feelings. Common defenses against shame include controlling, blaming, criticizing or feeling superior to others.

Repressed shame and guilt cause a lack of trust in others and a deep breach or separation from your true self. Patterns of dysfunctional behavior in a person's life usually indicate a strong internal shame core. Lack of intimacy and connection to others indicates a lack of trust. Engaging in excessive use of alcohol and drugs may be an indicator of hidden shame. Engaging in unhealthy behaviors that society frowns upon creates even more shame. Feelings of shame are a threat to the integrity of the self.

Internalizing Shame: Doing a Number on Yourself

Your Shameful Part convinces you that you are defective and do not deserve recovery. Someone else may have hammered shame into you, eroding your original sense of self. Who called you stupid when you were a child? Who told you that you would never amount to anything? Who criticized and cursed at you so that you hung your head in shame?

Kids often become what they are told by parents. This is the Self-Fulfilling prophecy. Some part of you may have bought into pessimistic programming. Children who have been highly criticized by others often internalize the Inner Critic. They carry around the Inner Critic who scolds them and always gives bad reviews on their behavior.

Stop Beating Yourself Up Emotionally

Now that you are in charge, do you carry out others' old role of heaping on the criticism? You can break into that negative self-fulfilling prophecy. So, what do you say to beat yourself up?

> "I'm bad. I'm so dumb
> I'm a screw up so I'll act like one…
> I'm stupid. I'm just a rotten person.
> I can't stand these bad feeling so I'll just have a few beers."

Shame needs to be addressed if you are to have a healthy, happy life. Grownups can choose who they become, and you are a grownup now. Fire your Inner Critic who beats you up. Reject that old negative prophecy of "You are dumb, stupid, a slut, a drunk, etc." Hire a Kinder Critic that gives you better reviews. Get one that sees the brighter side of who you are and gives you credit for your hard work. Goodbye Inner Critic, hello Higher Power.

Then make amends for beating yourself up. Be on the lookout for shame so you can challenge it at every turn. See your glass as half-full rather than half-empty. Cancel or terminate those destructive expectations that have been set up in your mind. They are lies that drag you down.

Perhaps the Biggest Denial of All Is Denial of Your Very Own Self!

Perhaps you know all about the different forms of denial, but still don't get it. The cruelest denial of all is thinking, "Yeah, yeah, yeah, I get it, but I can still use!" This is the biggest Con talk of all. You know everything you need to know but you still think you can get away with drinking or drugging. This way of thinking is a form of treacherous pride that refuses to know the true understanding of you and your addiction. It agrees to believe this lie of "I know, but I can still use...." to keep you from becoming who you truly are.

This is truly betrayal. Betrayal of yourself by your Inner Con.

The Duplicity of the Con

Understand the subtlety of this matter here. Alcohol and drug use are merely metaphors of how you throw yourself away. See how disastrous errors of thinking will ruin your life. In this mind-set, cravings will come up, and then off you go to worldly things that alter your mood and your reality.

Attack this cruel Con talk vigorously. Don't participate in its betrayal. Don't ignore Con talk. Meet it head on. Step up and see everything associated with your addiction as forms of the lie in your life. View the boredom, guilt, shame, desperation, desire, relief, and the highs for what they are. They are merely barriers in your mind that you have set up to keep you from finding your Truth.

5

ACCEPT THE TRUTH ABOUT YOURSELF

Accept the Truth About Yourself

If your life has been out of control due to your using, then you are an addict. If you harbor this dreadful denial about yourself that you can go back and use, stop and yell:

"THIS REALLY MEANS THAT I CANNOT ENGAGE IN MY ADDICTION EVER AGAIN. IF I WANT TO FIND MYSELF, I CAN NEVER GO BACK TO USING. I CAN NEVER USE ALCOHOL OR DRUGS AGAIN! I WANT TO LIVE MY TRUTH. I'LL FIND A WAY TO RECOGNIZE THAT I CAN NEVER USE AGAIN. I WANT THE TRUTH MORE THAN ANYTHING!"

Then smile at yourself for knowing your truth!

Then really get it. Get the reality of it. Know from the deepest level of your being that it is a "given" in your life that you can never, ever return to your addiction. This is your gospel Truth. You can do what it takes to live your Truth.

Your Truth is waiting to set you free.

Your Inner Con Has Low Frustration Tolerance

Hey! Life is stressful. Somehow we all seem to end up in the fast lane! Watch how you build up that volcano of stress until it turns into desire for using. You can become a reactor to crisis instead of taking action on your own behalf if you don't build relaxation into your life.

Stuffing feelings creates more internal stress. Avoiding talking about your problems with your friends keeps it all bottled up. Put off doing anything about the pressure and it intensifies. You create more stress, and then impulsively react to it. The pressure builds and you can't tolerate internal discomfort. The "wantas" slide down into the "I gotta get the high right now!" You demand any fix that takes away the pain and emptiness.

Under high stress, you might forget about all those positive tools for taking good care of yourself. Stuffing or running from uncomfortable feelings makes them grow into monsters! Suppressed feelings become volcano size, which then must blow up.

Your Inner Con Narrows Your Choice Field Down to Going After Your Addiction

Obsessive thoughts narrow your choices down to the wrong one. Your mind can get stuck in a rut saying the same negative thing over and over. Watch out if you hear yourself say, "I gotta have it now!"

Low frustration tolerance increases as stress piles up in your life. Stuffing your bad feelings encourages the belief of "I can't deal with this except by using...."

You **always** have more choices than you think. If you think you have only one choice, you are conning yourself again big time! Having only one choice of running toward your addiction full force is like wearing horse blinders. Open up your choice field. Life is never about having only one choice.

The Con Is a Tyrant of Fantasy Who Plays Bad Tricks With Your Mind!

Under every addict is a tyrant of fantasy who lives to party, party, party! This seductive part messes with your mind and depicts captivating scenes of "use." Your Inner Tyrant of Fantasy anticipates relief from the withdrawal symptoms and negative moods. It romanticizes the positive aspects of your addiction.

Your mind can paint tantalizing pictures of how great it was for you to indulge in your addiction. Your Tyrant of Fantasy thinks only of the fun associated with using. It fantasizes on the beginning of the use, not the end. It remembers only the fun that was associated with using. This tempting part overemphasizes the euphoria of drug use. The good old days are glamorized and idealized.

Your Inner Con Blocks Out and Minimizes the Negative Memories of Using

Amnesia for the bad times can set in. The severe negative consequences of those using times become fuzzy. You forget the hangovers, the missed days of work, the shame of the DUI and the wrecked car. You block out the disappointed look on your child's or spouse's face. You forget your discouragement and the broken promises to yourself. There's a false positive expectation of using. Your Con tells you to go for the high, the buzz, and the thrill. And so, you gloss over the bad, the desperate and the ugly.

Then Your Inner Tyrant starts looking around for anything that will take you out of your misery. Desire and desperation build up convincing you that the only solution is to use. This is one time where you should not focus on the positive, but hold those negative consequences of using in your mind.

Your Con Says to Go to Your Other Addictions

Addictions are rarely singular. If you have one addiction, you probably have others. These are called cross addictions. Many people move from one addiction to another. Other addictions may lie under your primary addiction. There are interchangeable links between craving for one drug or activity and cravings for others.

Cross addictions happen when you go for other substances and activities when you can't have your major drug of choice. So what is your second drug of choice? And your third?

Cross addictions can affect how you think so you will act on your craving. You substitute other risky behaviors to alter emotional cravings and negative moods. Instead of dealing with your problems, you seek something else to self-medicate. Watch that you just don't start going from one negative addiction to another.

6

FIND YOUR STUCK POINTS DURING STRESSFUL TIMES

Watch Out! You May Get Stuck When You Are Stressed

A stuck point is a complicated time where temptations for relapse loom large. You may recognize that you are stuck or you may lapse into denial and maladaptive coping and using. Being stuck is caused by a lack of skills in knowing how to interrupt addictive preoccupations. It may come from your lack of confidence to complete the program. It may come in despairing, "what's the use?" type of thinking.

Monitor yourself for feeling like you are in a rut. You can identify those feelings, desires, sensations and thoughts that signal impending drug use! Then you can focus your energy on finding those relapse prevention skills needed to get you out of your rut and back on track.

Radar! Radar! Physically Pooped? Stress Alert!

Notice when your resources for healthy living become depleted. During stressful times, people often revert to their most dysfunctional behavior.

Urges and cravings can become overpowering during difficult times. When there is more stress in your life, you probably do not take good care of yourself: you're likely to seek that substance or activity and try to fill up that hole of feeling bad and not being good enough.

During times of becoming depleted, stress will begin to build. This is a crucial time for you. During stressful times, people often revert back to their destructive addictions. Stress can cause you to cope less and less well. During times when you feel overwhelmed, watch out. This is the time to pull out all your good mental health tools and use them.

Watch Out for Bad Habits That Entice You to Relapse:

- Not taking care of emotional needs
- Not taking care of physical needs
- Pushing your body to exhaustion
- Stuffing feelings/not confronting others
- Allowing irritability to build up
- Withdrawing and isolating from others
- Withdrawing into the silent treatment
- Personalizing and internalizing anger
- Dwelling on intrusive negative thoughts
- Having to be perfect or expecting others to be perfect

Be on Alert for Those Lifestyle Stressors that Are Setups for Relapse!
- Junk food diet
- Someone you love using alcohol/drugs
- Poor stress management

- Diagnosis of Illness/Chronic Illness
- Not getting enough exercise
- Conflict or fighting
- Loss of emotional support/friends
- Financial stressors
- Poor boundaries with others/feeling used
- Constant worry
- Death in family/close friend
- Arrest or charge for serious offense
- Divorce or marital separation
- Marriage or marriage reconciliation
- Serious sickness or injury to self/other
- Excess use of sweets
- Child in trouble at home/school/with the law
- High level of exercise or nicotine can also trigger cravings

Returning to Your Addiction Will Cause More Stress

Your return to alcohol/drug use will cause you stress! Call a friend. Get a massage. Get things off your overloaded plate. Do whatever you have to do or pay whatever you have to pay to get the stress out of your life.

Dealing with the stress directly is much cheaper in the long run than going back to bad habits. Whether you use to avoid the stress or use to relax the stress, using *always creates* more stress!

Use Your Creative Imagination to Think About the Negative Costs of Your Addiction

One handy mental health tool is to identify and focus on the worst consequence of relapse. Picture yourself using and tell yourself, "If I use once, then I will…. If I start…, then I'm susceptible to doing one after another after another."

Remember that you have the capacity to keep using until you're out of control. Break into that conning lie that you can stop after just one…bring in your creative imagination to picture yourself hitting bottom. See your life veering out of control. Visualize yourself in your own personal gutter. Keep reminding yourself of the insatiable addict within that can't stop and keeps on using.

Imagine yourself confronting and defeating those Con words. See yourself going past desire, lies and the cravings. Reject those drug related environmental cues. Refuse to listen to that tyrant of fantasy clamoring that biases your decision-making. Visualize yourself as a powerful person taking charge of your irrational thinking. Remember those feelings of humiliation when you were caught in the throes of your addiction.

It took you this much effort to get your addictive behavior under control. Don't waste your sobriety on those calculating Con falsehoods. Tell yourself you don't want to blow it. Tell yourself that you are worth it.

7

CON WORDS OF IMPENDING RELAPSE

Con Words of Impending Relapse: Shades of Truth and Blatant Lies

Grandiose thinking to make you feel better than others is a favorite Con trick. Watch for these boasting words of that cunning Con that tries to convince you that you can handle things all by yourself:

> "I'll never use again.
> I don't need a Twelve-step program.
> There are too many hypocrites in my recovery program so I won't go.
> I don't have as big a problem as others, so I don't need to go to meetings.
> Alcohol is my only problem.
> I don't need other people. I can do it all alone.
> I've got all the answers.
> I don't need to call my sponsor.
> I'm not like those other people at my recovery meeting.
> I'm cured now. I can quit working my program.

What the heck! I'll deal with the consequences when they come.
I can't take it anymore. One drink won't hurt."

The Siren Songs of Excess Will Try to Tempt You to The Rocky Shore of Addiction

Remember that first use of your drug of choice can trigger the uncontrollable desire for more. Picking up that first drink, joint or experience can render you powerless. Using can equal more using.

The cost extracted is losing youself in the process. Get out your mental health toolbox and search for the right one to break into the lies. If you hear yourself saying these things, run, do not walk, to the nearest meeting.

Take positive action immediately to deal with any deceitful Con reasoning! Recognize those scamming Cutoffs that set you up for failure. Analyze the negative stressors inside and outside that do you in. Write down the stressors that you worry about. Acknowledge your physical discomfort as a trigger for using. Immediately apply relaxation to your stressed out mind and body.

Call a friend who is calming and affirming of you. Ask them to breathe through it with you.

The Clamor of the Con Is Relentless. Just in Case You Haven't Gotten It by Now, Con Talk is...

Arrogant, badgering, beguiling, bellyaching, betraying, bitter, biting, boring, calculating, caustic, censorious, complaining, conspiring, corroding, critical, crooked, cruel, cunning, cursing, deceiving, dejecting, designing, disgruntled, disheartening, dishonest, dissatisfied, disapproving, disruptive, dogmatic, enticing, false, fault-finding, fickle, fraudulent, frustrating, grousing, grudgeful, grumbling, harsh, hindering, hostile, irritable, irritating, insufferable, lying, loathing, misleading, mortifying, obsessive, obstructive, pesky, perfidious, plotting, quarrelsome, resentful, restless, revolting, seductive, shaming, sickening, sneaky, sneering, stinging, stubborn, sulking, traitorous, treacherous, tricky, underhanded, undermining, unsavory, vexing, whining and wily.

Oh, yeah! That is how it is.

The Con Is Your Worst Enemy

Your Con can mask itself as the search for pleasure and release from pain. Its habitual harassment is enough to provoke a saint. It is an arrogant braggart, bantering and blustering, to corrupt your principles. It is a tricky, troublemaker that's full of spleen and bile. The chip on its shoulder is heavy and huge as it prepares for the double cross. It lurks and lies in wait to give you one bad time in the name of having a good time. Its afflictions feed your discomfort and troubles. Its negativity is perpetually ready to give you the third degree.

The Con is an ever-present nag that reminds you how you have been betrayed. It haunts you like the plague, always ready to step in and bend your purpose. It's always ready to dupe you and make one last ditch effort to get you to use. It sows the seeds of your discontent to get you to that desperate state of craving and using. It taunts, lies, cheats, and says anything to resist its own demise. It goes on the offensive to offer you gall and wormwood in the guise of feeling good.

The Con clamor is not to be put up with. The Con is all a lie. The Con voice is all illusion that gains power only when you listen to it. The Con is only a subpart of the totality of you, programmed in by the negativity of society. The Con is a carrier of all the disillusionment, disenchantment and grief that you have experienced in your life.

This Con is not who you are. It is only your attachment to attempt to avoid pain and seek false pleasure.

8

THE POSITIVE CAST OF CHARACTERS THAT CUT OFF THE CUTOFFS

The Positive Cast of Characters That Cut Off the Cutoffs

Fortunately you have all sorts of inner characters to help you achieve your goal of sobriety. These parts of you are positive and rooting for recovery. You are not in this noble fight all alone. You have many resilient parts of you that will help you stay straight. These life-affirming parts carry clever mental health tools to prevent relapse. They know just the right tools to cut off that nasty Con thinking.

Give power to these positive characters and you will give power to your life. It's tool time!

Find **Your Practical Part.** Breathe, step back then back off from the Con chatter. Access what is going on in your mind. Pride yourself on your practical nature. Realize that your lying Con is trying to hoodwink you and take over. Face your desire to use and choose to do something else.

Ask yourself what needs to be done from a practical view, and then do it.

Fire up **Your Inner Cheerleader.** Give yourself a pep talk: "I can deal with this. I handled this last time. I can beat the cravings. I got through the bad time before. I'm in charge here, not my cravings."

Ask **Your Inner Procrastinator** to help you out. Postpone those cravings. Put off thinking about using. Ride the tide of cravings and get on to something else. Chant, "Ride the wave! Ride the wave!"

Your Inner Distracter can woo you elsewhere. Get busy. Change your mental channel. Get out your mental health tool kit. Get your mind on your prevention tools to keep from thinking about using. Remember what has worked in the past to get you through the craving.

Have **Your Inner Drill Sergeant** yell, "Move, move, move!" Respond with positive action. Move on. Get out of your lonely space. Leave any setting that promotes the substance or unhealthy activity.

Your Inner Problem Solver can nudge you to get some help. Ask yourself, "Who can I call to get me through this?" Call several people and talk the rough time through. Keep calling safe people to get through this danger zone. Foster a good support system for staying sober. You can talk out uncomfortable feelings with those you trust. Remember, we all get by with a little help from our friends.

Turn Denial Back on Its Heels: Use Turnabouts to Stop Your Negative Thoughts

Remember when you were a kid and twirled yourself around until the world looked differently? Turnabouts and turnarounds are things you tell yourself to get yourself back on the right track. Use them to cut off your nasty Cutoffs! Turnarounds are words that you say to turn your common sense back on!

Turnarounds remind you to take responsibility for the choices you make:

> "I'm the one who chose to go out partying.
> I'm responsible for my own anger. Hitting is wrong, no matter how angry I am.
> I make choices for myself no matter what anyone else chooses to do.
> No one can talk me into anything.
> I can choose recovery or being controlled by my addiction.
> Hey! I'm accountable for what I do."

Choosing Responsibility and Feeling Good About It

Give up the charade of rationalizing, minimizing and justifying using. Your chance for happiness is connected to your ability to admit what needs changing in yourself. Catch yourself in the dishonorable act of evading personal responsibility. Use your sense of truth and honesty to own up to your mistakes and slips ups. Turn blaming around to your being answerable for the choices you make. Make your life accountable for your actions and watch how your self-esteem soars!

It feels good to be responsible for making good choices for your life.

Remember to Remember

If your mind starts messing with you about how great using is, remember to remember. Use the mental health tool of remembering the truth of how miserable you were when using. Keep your mind on the negative consequences of your addictive behavior.

Don't kid yourself. Don't pull an Inner Con. Remember the bad things about using. Remember how you kept your life in turmoil by chasing your addiction. If your addiction didn't work in the past, it won't work for you now. If it was bad for you in the past, it won't work for you in the future.

Remember the important things. Valuing yourself and having pride in the choices you make is better than choosing addictions. Remember how satisfying a life free from addiction is. Remember who you are.

Remember to remember.

Playing It Straight: Stop Playing Con Mind Games

Your Con hates congruence. Congruence is the exact opposite of conning. It is straight communication, being in touch with your feelings and refusing to play mind games with yourself or others. Feelings, body language, facial expression, voice tone and posture are the same when you are congruent. You stay in context with what is going on and clarify facts and state opinions as such. You state your feelings and listen to others' feelings. You listen at a deep level trying to stay connected to the topic at hand. You can feel good about yourself as you problem solve and try to get to the bottom of things.

Good self-esteem pops up all over the place as you live, breathe and speak congruently. So make a contract with yourself about honesty and integrity. Tell yourself, "I will do what it takes to respect and love myself. I am a worthwhile person who can speak my truth at this moment. I choose to stay centered and deal straight with others. I choose not to get caught up in dysfunctional communication."

Recovery Is Feeling Good About Who You Are

Recovery is a process of becoming more and more congruent. There is pride in being straight with yourself and others. Your self-esteem becomes invested in living a healthy, happy life free of the control of addictions. Your positive identity of who you are becomes identified with the sobriety priority.

You can't play the Con and be congruent at the same time. The idea is for you to become who you would like to be. Walk your talk.

In recovery, keep that mental health toolbox handy! The recovery process is painful at times and is often accompanied with much confusion and clutter. But as you keep the goal of congruence foremost in your mind, you become more and more clear.

And if others start playing mind games, you pick up your marbles and go home.

Tool Box Instructions for Shaky Feelings

Feelings come and feelings go. Feelings are just that. Feelings. Feelings are meant to be felt!

So when your body is screaming and yelling, tell yourself:

"I am more than my uncomfortable feelings.
I can get through my anxious feelings.
I will ride out my craving period.
I won't let my negative thoughts and Cutoffs do me in!
I will experience my pain and discomfort by breathing into them.
I can live with the irritants and annoyances that life brings.
Feelings are just feelings. I don't have to give in to my shaky feelings."

Negative feelings are just that. They are negative emotional states, which represent unresolved pain that can be dealt with. Deny them any power over you. Don't give into bad feelings with thoughts of using. That will only make the cravings worse.

Tell yourself, "This too will pass. Feelings come and feelings go. I'm in control of my life when I deal with my negative feelings, body states and beliefs."

The Good News! Relaxation Inhibits Cravings

Ask **Your Higher Power** about adding relaxation tools to your life. Relaxation helps calm your mood and body, and it reduces those pesky cravings. You can't be tense and relaxed simultaneously.

For deep relaxation, learn practices that create tranquility like yoga, meditation and deep breathing. Join a Yoga, Tai Chi meditation or Chi Qong class to bring positive energies into your body. Learn Progressive

Relaxation, which is a quick method of tensing, holding, and relaxing specific muscle groups of the body. Learn the new Energy Therapies that give instant relaxation and help deal with cravings.

These techniques all work with the energies of your body that are out of balance when you are out of sorts. When you impose relaxation over tension, relaxation takes over.

9

THE LESSONS OF ADDICTIONS

The Lessons of Addictions

One way to look at life is to examine the lessons that are being presented to you. Addictions present you with important life's lessons. You are always being shown your lessons. Lessons are for learning. And they will be repeated until you get them. You do them until you get them right.

Mistakes are there for the correction. That's why pencils have erasers and computers have delete buttons. And that is why streets have U-turns! Sometimes our life just needs some "white-out" so we can correct our behavior.

Perhaps the greatest lesson of all is to learn to love yourself, warts and all. Your emotional well-being is dependent on your forgiving yourself and moving on with life.

Having to Take the Course Over

Unresolved pain can trigger cravings. Emotional pain is a signal that something in your psyche wants to be looked at. Did you grow up with drinking or drugging as a way of life, so you don't see anything wrong with it? You may be protecting old family secrets. Remember, "We are only as sick as we are secret." Look at the themes about addictions in your family and friends.

Ask yourself:

> "What negative beliefs did my parents and grandparents have?
> How has my mind become programmed by others about the need to party?
> How did addictive behavior in my home (or lack of it) affect how I see myself?
> What Cutoffs did I hear growing up?
> How did my parents deny looking at their own character defects?
> What erroneous beliefs about using did I pick up from my friends?
> Who is in charge here?"

What You Resist Examining Will Persist in Your Life

What you identify with becomes your reality. What you addict to becomes your certainty.

What you addict to becomes your Hell.

What you resist, persists. Symptoms of emotional pain are the "Yoo Hoos" to call your attention to get help. People who grow up in dysfunctional families have distorted ways of interacting with others. They develop ways of negative coping with stress that are not conducive to happy living. The question is not whether drinking or drugging is right or wrong. The question is "What has your addictive behavior done to the quality of your life?" Interrupt those core scripts about addictions that you have inherited from your family.

Addictions Appear to Work!

Umm…Sort of. Addictions temporarily distract you from problems, anxiety and pain. There are subtle benefits that you may unconsciously associate with your using. You may use them to feel connected to people, to punish your parents or spouse, or to avoid dealing with life situations. Maybe you use them to keep from growing up.

So addictions can appear to work. The key word here is "*appear.*" Addictions *appear* to work because stress, boredom and anxiety are temporarily subsided. However, your problems that created the stress, boredom and anxiety never get worked out. So they really don't work and they create bigger problems.

Addictions Don't Work!

Addictive substances and behaviors only produce a temporary tranquilizing effect or a high. Addictions cause your stress load to increase. They boomerang and come back around and knock you down. The high and good feelings fade and you feel worse than before. Your life zooms out of control, making you feel worse than ever after using.

Negative addictions are the big steal. They are the "empty, feel good" substances and activities that provide a short-term fix. They are used to quell the pain, the hunger, ailments or emptiness in life. The altered state that addictions provide is a short-term fix that doesn't last. Then you are left to live with the identity loss. Addictions are the way you say, "I don't want to be me!"

So check out your Con talk. Listen to what the talk tells you. There may be hidden needs being met through your addictive behavior that you can get met in healthier ways.

Be conscious about whatever benefits you perceive for choosing to use. Figure out at least ten reasons for choosing your addiction. Then take the strongest reason and list other things you could do to get the same results. Go to the next reason for using and list other things you could do instead. And then go to the next reason and do the same thing.

10

TO BE HUMAN IS TO BE ADDICTIVE

To Be Human Is to Be Addictive

Human beings are addictive creatures. We all have addictive personalities: craving and attachments are part of being human. We are all addicted to something. We addict to powerful preferences, intense attachments and strong opinions. We attach to lifestyles, reputations, ways of thinking, habits, and creature comforts. We addict to feeling good and trying to avoid distress. We have strong ideas, things and situations for which we strive to uphold. People seek out addictive behavior to deal with their stress.

Buddhist psychology says that it is the nature of humans to be attached and addicted. Much suffering comes from attachment to things that are not good for us. Some things that we are addicted to are destructive to our body, mind or spirit.

So since we are beings who suffer addictions, it would serve us well to examine what we addict to!

Negative Addictions Are Robber Barons

The negative addictions are those excessive behaviors that rob you. They steal from your pocketbook while you are unaware. They steal you blind, leaving you with a diminished sense of self. They decrease self-esteem and destroy your body. They include all those maladaptive ways you have learned to deal with stress. These are the "empty feel-good solutions."

Negative addictions eventually decrease the good chemicals in the brain that are associated with relaxation. They create an artificial high that over time decreases healthy brain functions. They include those harmful activities, fueled by that ever-present Con, which only add to your depression and anxiety level.

A Life Spent Chasing "Empty Feel-Good Solutions" Is a Singly Focused Life.

Negative addictions narrow your life choices down to the alcohol or drug pursuit. During using, there may be other people around, but the addictive high isolates you from others. There may be drinking/drugging/gambling buddies. Negative addiction pursuit can falsely gratify your need for companionship. Negative addictions are engaged in as a way of reducing the stress that you feel, however, these choices end up causing much more stress in life.

The Con cunningly keeps you from activities in life that bring true satisfaction. Negative addictions can create a temporary feel-good solution, while creating life pain and chaos. Eventually they undermine your health or your bank account. The guilt that you feel for overindulging devastates your self-esteem. Empty feel-good solutions that take you away from your values and standards do you in. They can cause people you love to give up on you. They disconnect you from family and your pride in who you are. Happiness is never found in a bottle, a drug or an activity that consumes you.

Since It's Our Nature to Be Addictive, Why Not Choose Positive Addictions?

It serves us well to examine what we attach to. So if we must be addicted; why not become addicted to things that help create happiness?

Beneficial addictions reduce stress and decrease anxiety, depression, irritability and anger. They are activities that are inexpensive or free that do not harm your body. Positive addictions include activities and achieving personal goals that strengthen you and bring satisfaction.

Positive addictions add to your life. They increase your self-esteem. They do not subtract from you and your personal resources. They hook into the pleasure center in your brain and increase those good brain chemicals called endorphins. The good addictions provide buffers against bad moods, psychological distress and failure.

Positive addictions enhance your relationship with yourself, your loved ones and with something greater than yourself.

Positive Addictions Include:

- Support and intimacy from caring friends who are there for you
- Exercise, movement, sports, Yoga, Tai Chi
- Deep breathing, meditation, prayer and relaxation exercises
- Experiencing the openness and acceptance of our furry and feathered friends
- Music (Mozart, Beethoven, and Gregorian chants) puts you in an altered state of mind
- Any activity, such as gardening, hiking, biking, or camping
- Writing or journaling
- Self-help groups
- Express feelings when upset and identify the triggers that set you off
- Exciting/spontaneous activities/travel
- Spiritual activities and rituals
- Social service activities and volunteer work
- Family activities and good, loving relationships
- Laughing at your oh-so-human self doing those oh-so-human things
- Any passionate activity that doesn't steal you blind, hurt your body, or damage your relationships

Natural Highs and Holy High

Natural and Holy Highs are sensory experiences that prepare you for release of tension and stress. They may utilize altered states of prayer, meditation, humming and ritual to give you a deeper understanding and meaning for your life. They can involve movement, dance, drumming, and breath work to prepare for spiritual opening.

Natural and Holy Highs lift you up and energize your body, mind and spirit. Sacred Highs fill up that void within with the substance of Spirit, not the substances of addictions. They add to your life, enhancing your sense of well-being.

Surrendering your problems to something greater than yourself creates a Holy High. Turning your problems and cravings over and offering them up can give you a sense of purpose in your life. You cannot be content until you are able and willing to add the Natural Highs to your life. Cultivate the daily Holy High habit of finding things in your life for which you are grateful.

Should You Slip into Relapse, Call Up Your Neutral Observer

Boredom can be a daily tempter to return to the wild life. A life chasing addictions becomes routine, robotic and unconscious. You cut out other interesting activities, so life becomes stagnant. Transform yourself from being unconscious, robotic and reactive into staying present in the moment and dealing with whatever presents itself before you.

Mindfulness can help you learn to be awake and alive in the present moment. Mindfulness is a form of attentional training that focuses on thoughts, feelings and reactions. You learn to watch your reactions instead of reacting to them. You learn to disidentify with negative emotions rather than be captured by them. Your Neutral Observer can help you find the deeper, more subtle truth inside of yourself.

The Neutral Observer Is a Pretty Cool, Wise, Old Sage Who Practices:

- Detaching from strong emotions and judging
- Calming down that **Inner Critic** who is hell-bent to beat you up
- Collecting the relevant information about what happened
- Feeling concern, yet thinking calmly and refraining from beating yourself up
- Going above the situation to give you a different perspective
- Analyzing the feelings, thoughts, sensations and behaviors that set up the relapse
- Seeing setbacks and problems as opportunities to practice and grow
- Calling in **Your Higher Power** to support you with love through shaky times

Then quite characteristically, that Wise, Old Inner Sage goes for the shock treatment. He gives you a whack on the head or a kick in the butt to get you back on course. Then Your Higher Power comes in and reminds you that your expert is within. With Your Higher Power, you can turn your problems over and surrender them.

11

THE PERIOD AFTER RELAPSE IS A CRITICAL TIME

The Period After Relapse Is a Crucial Time

A slip back into your addictions can quickly turn into a downward spiral unless you intervene immediately. Beating yourself up after a relapse is a way to keep yourself so depressed that you'll keep using. Con voices become powerful when you are down and out and disappointed with yourself. Backslides are golden opportunities for the tricky Con to gain strength.

The Con comes in with bad news to persuade you how rotten you are. It sneers at you and tells you that you don't deserve sobriety. The Con plays up your backsliding to point out how weak you are. It cunningly says, "You blew it so you might as well keep on using." That devious Con convinces you that it was dumb to think that you could make it sober. It feeds on your shame and embarrassment because you broke your promise to yourself. Shame comes up making you feel so bad that you'll give up your goals and aspirations of remaining clean and sober.

Yes, Yes, You Too Can Break the Cravings/Poor Self-Esteem Chain!

You can jump into the cycle at any place to break into its destructive pattern. Be aware of negative patterns that you go into when things feel overwhelming in your life.

Stay out of the Cravings/Poor Self-Esteem Chain that leads to going back to your drug of choice!

Here is the cycle:

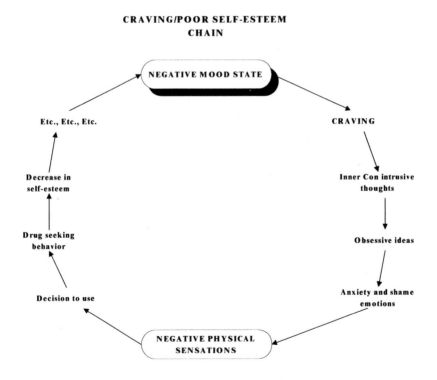

**CRAVING/POOR SELF-ESTEEM
CHAIN**

NEGATIVE MOOD STATE

CRAVING

Inner Con intrusive
thoughts

Obsessive ideas

Anxiety and shame
emotions

NEGATIVE PHYSICAL
SENSATIONS

Decision to use

Drug seeking
behavior

Decrease in
self-esteem

Etc., Etc., Etc.

Pin that Inner Con to the Ground

Break into the Cravings/Poor Self-Esteem Chain at the earliest time you can! Recognize the cravings as normal and decide not to act on them.

So if you feel tempted to listen to Con talk when you are having cravings, give yourself a pep talk:

> "Right now, I'm having a craving.
> It's okay to have cravings. Most people have cravings.
> Cravings are normal for me.
> Cravings do not equal who I am. I am not my craving.
> Just because I'm having a craving doesn't mean something is wrong with me.
> I crave because I feel anxious about something.
> This is normal. It's just a craving. I don't have to act on it.
> I will not do or use something that is harmful to me just because I have cravings.
> There are better ways to take care of my boredom or anxiety than using.
> No matter what, no matter how bad it gets, I don't have to use.
> I can do something else instead.
> This, too, will pass.
> Cravings will go away if I don't use.
> I ride the wave of cravings and get past them.
> I can change my physical setting.
> I can get up and do something.
> I leave this place of craving.
> I can do what it takes to take care of ME!
> I take charge of my life.

I choose to feel good about myself!
Now what worked for me last time?"

Relapses Are for Learning

Slip ups are a golden opportunity for you to learn more about yourself. After a relapse, analyze where you went wrong so you can change it. Discover those Con statements that gave you permission to start down that road to nowhere. Take back your control from those doom-predicting parts of yourself. The period after acting out with your drug of choice is lesson-learning time.

Relapses are for learning. Don't beat yourself up so that you throw in the towel and give up on your hard-earned sobriety. Use your energy to find out what went wrong and correct it. Take positive action to make a plan so that self-destructive Con won't gain control again. Apprehend those deadly tendencies within yourself to go down the wrong path. You are where you place your energy.

You can waste your energy by giving into Con talk and give yourself permission to keep using. Or you can place your energy into recovery and the sobriety priority. Where you put your energy after a relapse is a sweet, simple choice.

Get back on the wagon and continue with the parade of your life. Heading up your own parade is much more fun than being in the gutter.

Fear Is the Big Lie After Relapse

The sneaky Con lurks around within until you are bored, feeling down or anxious. Then it shouts, "Gimmee those things that make me feel good for a while." Addictions are born of fear that lies to you. They say, "I don't care what the cost is to my body, self-esteem, job, partner or children. Let me numb out this pain/thought/trauma with something that takes me away from the fear of not being enough. Just give me those "empty-feel-good solutions" for a while." One Big Lie is that you can continue to use without dire consequences.

Addictions separate us from our true self. When we feel separate from who we are, we experience guilt, shame, fear and judgment. Addictions create the feelings of being unworthy and unlovable.

Don't Give in to the Con's Lies: More Handy Self Talk

Keep adding more ideas to your tool kit for sobriety. Tell yourself:

> "This is not about willpower. It's only about getting through this next moment.
> I'll be better off if I don't give in. I better not…. So I can be better.
> If I do this, I fail. If I give in, I'll be sorry later.
> There is a way that I can get through this tough time. I will find the way.
> I'm putting the brakes on this craving before it breaks me.
> This is one lethal security blanket I don't want wrapped around me.
> I don't need that chaos, guilt and shame that using would send me back to.

I don't need this substance or activity of choice to make
myself okay.
What this time is about is finding a way to hang on to my
self-respect.
I'll go to a meeting or call my support people.
All I really need is to feel good about being in charge of
myself.
I've neglected my talents, values, work, family, friends and
myself.
Now it's time to neglect my addiction."

Fear Creates the Con Talk

Every single thought, feeling, sensation or behavior that you have either
comes from fear or love.

The sense of emptiness and separateness comes from the fear-based
part of the ego. Anger, hurt, sadness, grief, unhealthy desires, stubborn-
ness, anxiety are all fear-based. Cravings and the overwhelming desire
for addictive substances and activities are created by fear.

Fear is belief in lack. It is the belief that you lack something. Fear lives in
poverty consciousness. Fear is born of trauma, abuse or ridicule. As
anxiety, it reinforces itself with overindulgence. Addictions are a sign
that deeply hidden in your psyche is a fearful belief of your not being
worthy. The voice of the perfidious Con says, "I am not enough. I am
less than. I need something outside myself to make me feel complete."

Fear creates the addictions and compulsive behavior that interfere with
joyful living. Fear takes you out of who you are. Fear with the voice of

the Con is the seducer who sucks you dry. It seduces you back into the bottle, the drug or dangerous, obsessive activity. Fear is the Big Lie.

Shame Is the Shaper of Symptoms; But It is Also the Way Home

At some point in an individual's life, the old defenses to keep shame hidden away no longer work. Shame comes up. The person's life crashes around him. Hitting bottom and the resulting shame may take the person to a place of deep pain where he or she is ready to seek help.

One purpose of the negative emotion is to help you look at those aspects of yourself that are at odds with your deepest values. The anxiety around the painful past can be entered into and moved through.

Working Through Shame

Shame reduction work must be experiential. It cannot be released on an intellectual level. Shame can be released through confession and processing the original painful experiences. The original feelings can be understood and reframed to allow the shift of the shame energy. Deep feelings of vulnerability, fear and humiliation can be liberated in the presence of caring others.

Understanding how shame works helps release it. Cleaning out the global belief of "I am bad." takes time and exploration. It can be done with people who understand the process of shame release and are able to stay present with unconditional love. Laughter about one's predicament and humanness helps shift the shame energies.

The Paradox of Guilt and Shame

The paradox of the base emotions of guilt and shame keep you from knowing that down deep inside you there is a loving being. And yet the solution in releasing them is to get to the place of knowing "I am love."

The deep spiritual understanding is that no one can truly be harmed. The core negative beliefs of "I am a bad person. I am not safe. I am not enough. I will be rejected because I am unworthy. I will be abandoned." can be worked though.

Turning the shame over to something greater than oneself can negate those global beliefs of unworthiness. Touching into the higher aspects of oneself can help assure you that you are worthy of being loved. Self-esteem zooms upward as old layers of shame are released.

No easy task, but there it is.

12

THE PARADOX: THE CON POINTS THE WAY HOME

The Paradox: The Con Also Points the Way Home

Your Con is much more than the seducer and betrayer. This is another great paradox. What can potentially hurt you can also be your savior. The Con shows you where your weaknesses are. It shows you *where* to address the betrayal and pain.

Con talk comes forth as symptoms and erroneous beliefs to be worked out. As a signal, the Con shows how you deny and cover up the grief and pain in your life. It points out the areas of unhappiness in your life that can be worked through. That which defeated you can empower you, if you turn it back on itself.

Listen well to the words of the Con. The Con speaks the core negative scripts that you hold about yourself that beg for correction. Pull out your mental health toolbox and find those right tools for tricky times. When you hear yourself doing Con talk, ask, "Do I have a higher thought than that?" If you address the hurt and pain underneath the Con, you will find the path to recovery.

To stay clean and sober is to find our your identity. You will not only find yourself; you will have a great journey along the way!

Maturing Out—Letting the Addiction Go and Gaining Yourself

Rebellion wears thin when you stop giving in to the out-of-control, immature aspect of yourself. Your Rebel loses its power when you recognize how incomplete your user existence is. You observe how you are never being satisfied with how much you are using. You become aware of how you've lost faith in yourself. You find that you can no longer cop out and run from the distasteful realities that addictions bring. You identify how you've become dependent on outside stimulation rather than drawing from inner resources.

You are maturing out when you discover that rebellion has kept you from avoiding the decisions of life that brings true satisfaction. You recognize that you've postponed important developmental milestones in your life. You start to question the dependency-creating actions asking, "Is this all there is to living?" You recognize the payoffs for doing things differently, and you find pride in being responsible. You're ready to end the inner conflict and lay down those Rebel tools of war. You resolve to get on with the business of truly living instead of checking out. You gain genuine involvement in everyday activities that bring satisfaction.

The Biggest Lie of All

Maturing out of addictive behavior is getting rid of that irrational belief that you must feel good at all times. Feelings are meant to be felt, even the uncomfortable ones. You can learn to allow uncertainty and the unpredictability that life brings and find pride in facing the unknown. You mature out of your addictions as you know and live the possibility of gaining something better for yourself.

Integrity is doing those things that you believe in. As you mature out of your addictions you will find an internal respect for yourself.

Childhood is over. It's grow up time!

Depending on How You Do It, the Recovery Process is Heaven or It Can Be Hell

Your process is a psychological journey of becoming who you are and regaining your sense of self. You can find out who you are without the chaos of addictions in your life. It is a process of turning around and seeking aid to regain one's balance in life.

The practice of staying clean and sober can bring you more fun, spontaneity and freedom. It can take you to deep friendships and renewed relationships with those you love. The process of recovery is restoring your alliance with Your Higher Power and realigning with your soul's purpose.

Remember to trust the process. Trust the process. The journey will lead you to personal and spiritual growth. It will take you on an exciting adventure. You are in a process of becoming. After a while you begin to know that your life is such a lovely process. The template for growth is set in place. You are a Human Being in process.

For Successful Recovery, Trust Your Process

Making the Sobriety Priority is a lifelong, day-by-day process, which concentrates on the present, neither on the past nor the future. The first step in seeking help is to admit to the problem. Face the fear of the consequences that you have created in your life. Watch yourself when conflict and bad moods come up. Recognize your own negative response to a problem. Make the decision to stop acting in ways that hurt yourself and others. Feel good about making positive choices. Use pep talks to shut down the voice of the Con. Find satisfaction in learning to own your own behavior. Pride yourself on being congruent and straight with people. Keep looking for new healthy responses to old problems.

Practice the new positive language of recovery. Talk your program. Walk the talk. Go to meetings. Live your recovery plan. Find gratitude daily for all the beautiful things that life presents you. Practice, practice, practice the fine art of living your life with integrity.

13

FILLING THE VOID WITHIN

Filling the Void Within

The need for addictive release from pain and suffering is a search for Spirit. Carl Jung said that the craving for alcohol is equivalent to spiritual cravings. The Latin word *spiritus* has a dual meaning of alcohol and spirit. Addictive behaviors can come from a feeling of emptiness or a "hole in the soul." In a downward spiral fashion, addictions contribute to the increasing void of the individual. Addictive behaviors, done excessively, cheat you of your loving connections to others.

Addictions are an attempt to seek and to fulfill the desire for connection to something greater than you. The craving for Spirit is underneath the craving for any substance. The use of mind-altering chemicals and behaviors is an attempt to find the Divine. The seeking of mind-altering behaviors is a detour to your seeking transcendence, which only leads you down a blind alley.

Addictions are attachments that block your relationships with yourself, with others and with something greater than yourself. The "fill 'er up" of the empty hole in the soul can never be accomplished by an activity or substance. That's why the most effective recovery programs have a strong, spiritual basis. Connection to your spirituality and the deepest part of who you are is crucial to reduce cravings.

Recovery Includes Experiencing All as a Part of Life

You are now on the road to full recovery. Recovery is a path of direct experience. Feelings are meant to be felt. That is why they are called feelings. Even bad ones. Especially bad ones.

You can learn to experience all of life. The good days, the lows, the joy and also the pain. In experiencing the valleys of depression, you also get to experience the natural peaks and highs. In giving up the rush of addiction, you experience the natural, normal moods of life.

As you mature, you learn that it's okay to have internal discomfort. As you fill your life with positive addictions, meaningful experiences and Holy Highs, negative addictions lose their hold.

Healing Is Having a Relationship with Life

Addictions are about having a primary relationship with a bottle, a drug or an unhealthy activity. Your primary relationship should be with yourself and your loved ones.

Healing is available when you turn your addictions over to something greater than you are. Surrender with the intention to release that anything that does not fit your life anymore. Acceptance is having the situation or feeling be exactly the way it is. You hang out with boredom, anxiety or pain, instead of seeking relief or trying to change it. The trick is to allow bad feelings and learn to cope with them. You mellow out, knowing that you can handle discomfort.

The process of recovery is having a real relationship with all that life brings. Experiencing all. Showing up, suiting up and doing the work. Hard work to be sure, but you are worth it. The process of recovery is the path with heart.

Calling Higher Power. Higher Power, Come in Please!

You are enough! With all your connection to Your Higher Power and greater good in the Universe, you have all you need.

You are not unworthy. You do not need your addiction to feel good for a short time. Turn whatever ails you over to your Higher Power. You can break into those fear thoughts generated by your Inner Con. There is only one problem and one solution to that problem. No matter what the question, love is the answer.

You are more than your desires and cravings. You are more than the tension of your physical body. You are much, much more than your painful emotions. You are essence, longing to return to your true self.

You can only be as happy as you are able to find the love in every situation. Call in your Higher Power to show you the correct perspective. Your Higher Power will never fail you. You may fail Your Higher Power. Foster the attitude of appreciation of the small things in life. Nourish the habit of daily gratitude. Nurture the love within you that seeks growth and expansion.

Remember to Remember

Remember who you are. You are love. Whatever the fear, whatever the discomfort, whatever the craving, find the love solution. Remember to remember.

APPENDIX A

Learned Optimism

You can change those pessimistic statements that beat you up. Catch the negative thoughts flitting through your mind. Observe how they pull your mood down and make you feel helpless. Write down any negative statement that explains how you view life. Work this five-step process suggested by Martin Seligman in *Learned Optimism* to interrupt victim thinking.

1.   **Choose an Automatic, Negative Thought on Which to Intervene**

     I am so stupid.
     I don't have any will power. It's too hard to quit.
     I'm no good. I'm worthless.
     I give up. I can't deal with this.

2.   **Look for Contrary Evidence to the Recurring Negative Thought**

Remember and acknowledge all instances of how the statement is **not** true. Look at evidence that contradicts the negative belief.

Dispute the catastrophic things you hear yourself saying. Interrupt your pessimistic thinking. Argue with yourself about any negative belief!

Sometimes I make stupid mistakes, but I'm not stupid.
I've stayed sober this long. I can handle this pressure now.
I'm kind to my kids and give to charity. So I'm not too bad.
Maybe my badness is beating myself up!
Well, so far in life I've dealt with a lot worse.
I've handled a lot of difficult things and am still here.

3.   **Make Different Explanations About the Negative Belief**

Challenge your assumptions that pull you down. Interrupt the negative thought and give a new explanation.

My IQ is high enough; I beat myself up after a mistake. That's what's stupid.
Staying sober is worth whatever effort it takes.
I'll stop calling myself lazy when I don't want to do something.
I repeat "I'm no good" belief to beat myself up when I feel down.

I'll stop that victim thought and program in something positive.
My mother talked about being helpless and gave up. I won't repeat her errors.

4.   **Distract Yourself from Depressing Thoughts**

Stop ruminating on how deprived you feel. Do something, get busy, and turn on some happy music. Do anything other than sit around thinking depressing thoughts.

I'll change my mental channel. I refuse to dwell on this negative thought.
There I go perpetuating that error in thinking of how worthless I am.
How can I see this differently?
I refuse to give this negative thought free rent in my brain.
I have better things to think about.
I'm going to get up and do something to get my mind off of my stinking thinking.

5.   **Get Tough with Your Negative Thoughts and Craving Challenges**

Question any general assumptions and errors in thinking that keep you down in the dumps. Interrupt any of your "stinking thinking." Wrestle that Inner Con to the ground and make it say, "Uncle."

I won't give in to the belief that I must do my addiction or I'm miserable.

I refuse to see myself as deprived.

I'm not a victim. Victim is as victim thinks. I can interrupt my victim thinking.

I focus on all the good things going for me.

When I tell myself I can't cope with things, then I give up.

Giving in to negative thoughts really gets me down in the dumps.

I am as successful in life as I am able to control my negative thoughts.

APPENDIX B

Stages of Change

Take a leap of faith! Change is possible. Researchers have narrowed the change process down to five basic steps. No matter what the problem is, the process for change is the same.

Understand the process that you are moving though. When you start out on a journey, it helps to know where you are. To get from A to Z, you need a map. These stages or change and recovery provide you with a handy map.

Stages are just that: stages. You may go back and forth between the stages. Things may drag at times. Keep true to your map. Ask your Higher Power to spur you onward. With help from your Higher Power, you can move forward through the process of recovery.

James Prochaska, John Norcross and Carlo DiClemente describe their five stages for making lasting changes. Here is their basic model adapted for recovery issues. You can use their model for nailing down the recovery process.

1. Precontemplation: You are unaware or under aware of your problem with no intention for change.

2. Contemplation: You become aware of the problem.

You give serious thought about changing your behavior.

This is the "Maybe I should do something different" stage.

3. Preparation: You begin to have strong intentions about change for the future.

You consider lifestyle alternatives to addictive behavior.

You begin to take responsibility for your decisions and behaviors that are destructive to yourself and others.

You start to feel hopeful that you can do things differently.

4. Action: You set strong, but realistic standards for behavior.

You recognize and confront your own negative responses to problems.

You begin to modify behavior to overcome problems.

You find an environment that supports your changing.

5. Maintenance: You work to keep your behavior to the standard that you have set.

Recognition and reinforcement are needed as you continue your commitment to maintain gains.

Behavior change is easier if you arrange your environment to support your sobriety goals.

APPENDIX C

Stages of Recovery

Terry Gorski and Stephanie Brown give the stages that a person in recovery moves through. You are not unique. Others have made this journey before you. You can draw from their maps and their wisdom.

Remember using your drug of choice at anytime can reactivate the physiological, psychological and social progression of your addiction!

Transition Time

    Has a serious problem that is related to addictions.

    Believes that you are normal drinker or drug user capable of controlled use.

    Tries different strategies to control use.

    Experiments with quitting.

    Unsuccessfully tries to give up addictions.

    Tries to convince self and others that you can stop without outside help.

    Recognizes that safe use is no longer possible.

    Still using, feeling forced to go to treatment.

May be mandated by court, family or self to treatment.
Denial is still present.
Realizes that something different is needed.
Has resentment about having to quit.
Continues to manipulate self and others.
Experiments with twelve-step programs.
Partially goes with the program.
Does not have a full commitment for sobriety.

Stabilization

Sees need to establish an addiction free lifestyle.
May have acute withdrawal/post-acute withdrawal.
Stabilizes the crisis that prompted recovery efforts.
Gets a stable recovery environment.
Treatment is blocked by unresolved trauma and childhood issues.
Gets other diagnosis of depression/anxiety.
Starts to find tools to deal with cravings.

Early Recovery

There's a struggle to control behavior, and fear about failure.
Stops using drug or activity of choice.
Starts support groups and twelve-step programs.
Starts to learn about addictions and the recovery process
Must separate from friends who support using.
Realizes "It's a disease. And I have it!"
Starts to develop recovery-based values.
Starts self inventory.
Educates family & friends.
May become a drum-beating evangelist for AA.

Middle Recovery

Core addictive issues that are a setup for the desire for using come up.

Deals with unfinished business regarding past addiction such as—legal issues, health problems, job screwups and family problems.

Feels relief when some problems go away when using stops.

Identifies and starts to work on character defects.

Develops the recovery language, thinking, values, feelings and behaviors to replace old patterns.

Finds new ways to deal with stress and self-defeating behavior.

Finds a wise, supportive sponsor.

Asks for help when needed.

Makes a moral inventory and starts to clean up behavior.

Makes direct amends to people who have been hurt by your addictive behavior.

Late Recovery

Can be superficial and many get stuck here.

Goes to AA for fear of resuming drinking, but may never address deeper issues.

Examines values and goals programmed in by family, peers and culture.

Starts to deal with Cross Addictions.

Makes the sobriety priority in earnest.

Starts to seriously address core psychological issues of:

> Personality problems
> Abuse and abandonment
> Victim thinking
> Codependency
> Relationship problems

Current family issues
Old traumas
Anger and rage
Entitlements and the need to feel special (I deserve to use.)

Maintenance Recovery

Has a sense of purpose in recovery that helps created continued growth.
Addresses core psychological issues.
Addresses cross addictions—needs spare cross addictions
Continues working a program toward growth and intimacy with others.
Develops reliable techniques to deal with cravings and irrational thinking.
Keeps the wily Con thinking under control.
Deals with major adult-life transitions.
Self-esteem continues to grow based on a sense of accomplishment.
Focuses on service to others to give back what you have been given.
Works with Higher Power to make good life choices.
Gets a sense of pride and peace in life.

APPENDIX D

Brain Chemistry of Addictions

Addictions are treatable diseases that have both a psychological and biological basis. It is important to have a basic understanding of the biology of how addictions change your mood and actual brain functioning. The compulsive need for alcohol, drugs, eating disorders, compulsive behavior and mood swings can indicate out-of-whack brain chemistry.

Endorphins are those positive chemicals made by your brain that keep you in a pleasant or neutral state of mind. They are natural painkillers that are released when you go into a trance state. They are the chemical messengers known as neurotransmitters. These messengers communicate between the cells of the brain and shape mood.

Our emotions are regulated by these and other natural chemicals: Serotonin (calm), dopamine (happiness), norepinephrine (aggression) and oxytocin (social bonding.) When your neurotransmitters are out of balance, you feel depressed, anxious, unsatisfied or incomplete. Brain chemical dysregulation is a major culprit in addictions. And addictions can foster brain chemical dysregulation. It can become a nasty cycle.

Research is showing that people who addict or overeat may have fewer receptors for dopamine, a neurotransmitter that is connected to the pleasure center of the brain. People with fewer dopamine receptors are more vulnerable to seeking an outside high. Addictive drugs fire up the neurons and neurotransmitters that then move to stimulate the brain's pleasure circuit.

Sadly, the more alcohol or drugs that you use, the more you need. In chronic using, the brain's dopamine receptors can become destroyed so that larger and larger amounts of the alcohol or drugs are needed to get the same high.

Use Natural Escapes Instead of Chemical Ones

Using addictive substances can provide a brain chemical escape as an attempt to self-medicate to feel better. However, the reduction of tension after using is followed by feelings of guilt, anger, sadness or indifference. Chemical substances backfire and begin to play havoc with normal functioning brain chemistry. With the continual artificial stimulation of using alcohol and drugs, serotonin balance becomes more disrupted. Repeating the cycle of feeling bad and resorting to using more of the addictive substance creates more brain dysregulation.

Addicts often suffer from an undiagnosed low-to-high-grade depression or compulsive behaviors that may be related to brain chemistry. Research shows that some addicts reduce the possibility of relapse when they are given low doses of antidepressants. Successful recovery programs add positive activities that create positive chemicals in the brain. Engaging in challenging activities which demands personal commitment enhance happiness.

Go to your public library or on-line on the Internet to learn more about natural ways to regulate your brain chemistry to create healthy brain function. New natural ways to work with the neurotransmitters in the brain are being discovered. There is a new field of research linking addictions and allergies. Keep reading in the addictions and brain research area to be current in these fields. Check out the natural supplements that help regulate stress and mood. Follow the research that is focusing on the use of medications for assistance with staying sober.

Exercise is an extremely effective way to increase the dopamine levels and increase the number of dopamine receptors in the brain. And remember, laughter is one of the best ways to naturally stimulate the brain.

APPENDIX E

Non-substance Addictions

Most people think of alcohol or drugs when they think of addictions. But potentially anything can become addictive if it has the ability to change your mood for the better, however temporary. A recent study showed that brain activity of gamblers hoping to win at roulette are similar to the brain activity of people while they take cocaine and morphine.

Non-substance addictions are compulsive habits of dependence that soothe feelings of personal inadequacy. Non-substance addictions include any activity that produces satisfying states of high arousal. These out-of-control behaviors often give you an escape hatch from the blahs and the ho-hum life.

Some activities aren't normally inherently bad in themselves within reasonable amounts of use. But if done in excess to gain the predictable high, they can become obsessive. You sacrifice what you cherish most in order to continue the unhealthy fixation that pumps you up. You may even act out in an attempt to block out the very pain of your addiction. You may gravitate toward them in an attempt to reduce stress, however, they end up causing you more stress. Non-substance addictions include any unhealthy behavior that dominates your thinking and subsequently your life.

Non-substance addictions consist of any adrenalin-producing behaviors that take over your life. So whatever consuming activity you engage in to alter mood can become your "drug of choice." Non-substance addictions interrupt your sense of not being complete or satisfied. They include any activity or love object that enlivens and energizes you. Your body produces endorphins that temporarily boost your mood during the desired experience. You become overcharged and literally hooked on your own body chemicals.

Risky Behavior

Non-substance addictions include any normal behaviors that are taken to the extreme to gain the rush: Preoccupation with a person, work, romance, eating, shopping, gambling, sex or compulsive use of the Internet. Out-of-control sexual exhilaration can be classified as addictive. This includes excessive self-stimulation, affairs, exhibitionism, voyeurism, obscene phone calls, or pornography. Other non-substance addictions are risky novel activities that charge your energy and turn on your brain chemicals. These include an obsession for crisis and chaos, stealing, shoplifting, abuse and fighting or other unlawful behavior that brings an adrenalin high.

In non-substance addictions as well as the chemical ones, the need for the addictive experience intensifies. The danger signal is the obsessive way the activity or person becomes your narrow-minded focus. The relationship with the addiction becomes a priority more important than family, friends, and work. You go for the temporary pleasure rather than the deeper qualities of normal, intimate relationships.

Non-substance addictions entangle you in a way of life. They keep you caught in shame as they take over your mind and the context of your life. Dependency on the high increases, like all addictions, destructive activities create a cycle of shame driven and shame-creating behavior. Your self-regard becomes lost in the process of seeking those feel good activities.

APPENDIX F

Energy Psychotherapies

Energy Therapies are new techniques that are highly effective in treating addictions and correcting negative beliefs about the self by working with the body's energy. When there has been pain in a life and accompanying strong emotions, the Energy Therapies are the best way I've found to reduce old hurts and erroneous thinking. And as continuing hurts accumulate, stress becomes a way of life. Emotional ouchies build up!

These Energy Therapies work with the body's energy system and relieve emotional pain. They provide release of anxiety, insight and changes of negative beliefs. They produce shifts in the body's energy and biochemistry. Many of them are based on the meridian theory of Chinese acupuncture and use acupressure.

You can learn to apply some of these techniques at home on yourself! They are effective for stress, confusion, anxiety, phobias, depression, Post Traumatic Stress Syndrome, guilt, physical pain and enhancing performance in skills. And of course for coping with the stress or boredom that people with addictions have!

Some of these are new controversial therapies because they are not yet proven by research, but they are extremely effective. There are thousands of innovative therapists the world over using these techniques and who are dancing with excitement at the efficiency and rapidity of relief from symptoms that the Energy Therapies bring.

Go to these websites to check out these innovative Energy Therapy approaches. Most of these websites will list clinicians trained in the technique. Most clinicians who are trained in one of these techniques are cross-trained in the others.

Emotional Freedom Techniques (EFT)
Gary H. Craig
P.O. Box 398, The Sea Ranch, CA 95497
(707) 785-2848
http://www.emofree.com
http://www.emofree.com/addiction.htm

Gary Craig's website provides in-depth information on incorporating EFT into one's life. The Emotional Freedom Technique is easy to learn to tap on specific acupressure points. Inexpensive videotapes are available for purchase so you can learn to use this procedure on your own. The website features the "Palace of Possibilities," an extended set of essays on living well, eliminating unconscious obstacles to success plus pages on the use of EFT with addictions. EFT is a highly effective way to release Inner Con beliefs.

Eye Movement Desensitization and Reprocessing (EMDR)
Francine Schaperio, Ph. D.

P.O. Box 51010
Pacific Grove, CA 93950-6010
831-372-3900
http://www.emdr.com

EMDR uses rapid eye movements while processing emotions and uncomfortable body states to bring relaxation and relief. There is considerable research on the effectiveness of this technique.

Callahan Techniques, Ltd.
Roger Callahan, Ph. D.
78-816 Via Carmel
La Quinta, CA 92253
760-564-1008
http://www.tftrx.com

The Callahan Techniques, formerly called Thought Field Therapy, offers patterns of tapping on acupressure points and using eye movements to release stress, depression, anger, guilt and past and current trauma. It can be used to break into negative thought patterns and Inner Con talk. Dr. Callahan has a videotape on using his technique to quell addictions.

Tapas Acupressure Technique (TAT)
Tapas Flemming
P.O. Box 7000-379
Redondo Beach, CA 90277
877-TAT-INTL (828-4685) U.S. only
http://www.tat-intl.com

The Tapas Acupressure Technique is an accelerated information processing technique, useful in the treatment of traumatic stress, addictions,
allergic reactions, and fixed negative emotional states. It can be used
with stress and anxiety that accompany the wanting to return to using
addictive substances. TAT is a gentle technique using self-touch that is
based on concepts from Traditional Chinese Medicine.

Spiritual Kinesiology: Getting Though to Your Soul
Phillip and Jane Mountrose
Holistic Communications
P. O. Box 279
Arroyo Grande, CA 93421-0279
1-800-644-5437
www.gettingthru.org

This approach, which is taught by videotapes and their book, uses
imagery, muscle testing, anchoring and collapsing negative beliefs and
feelings by connecting you to your soul. Their website includes a free
spiritual newsletter sent out by email.

APPENDIX G

Resources

Under many addicts is flaming codependent behavior! My best-selling book, *The Doormat Syndrome*, is back in print again. You can read pages of *The Doormat Syndrome*, which is about codependency, learning to speak your truth, humor and spirituality at the iUniverse.com website
http://books.iuniverse.com/viewbooks.asp?isbn=0595160603&page=1
The Doormat Syndrome is available from iUniverse.com for $12.95.

Got Mads? Get 'em out! Check out my award-winning website on anger management at *http://members.aol.com/AngriesOut/index.htm*

The Angries Out web pages have won numerous national awards from mental health, parenting, teacher education, spirituality and art organizations. It features many articles about anger containment and management and the *Ask the Lady Who Knows About Mads* and *Here's How I Stopped My Mad Attack*. And you can post your amends on the *I'm Sorry I Hurt Someone* page. You can also get information about my free psychospiritual newsletter at the website.

For different self assessment tests on addiction that are presented on-line go to
http://silk.nih.gov/silk/niaaa1/publication/instable.htm

Information for women on their specific recovery issues during the sobriety process can be found at *http://www.womenforsobriety.org/*

NOTES ABOUT MY CON

NOTES ABOUT MY CON

About the Author

Lynne Namka, Ed. D., a psychologist who helps individuals with personal and spiritual growth issues, is the author of *The Doormat Syndrome*, a book on codependency and *The Mad Family Gets Their Mads Out, and How to Let Go of Your Mad Baggage*, available from her award-winning website at *http://members.aol.com/AngriesOut/index.htm*

"Of the many books I've reviewed about addiction relapse in the past 30 years, this is the best. Dr. Namka identifies brilliantly that a recovering addict's self-defeating self-talk is a seductive internal "Con," who is a skilled little liar, but doesn't represent the sum of the recovering person. That means that relapse is a choice, not a need. She shows with empathy, clarity and humor that we have a range of other options to choose from, she shows, and helps us to identify and use them."

Audrey DeLaMartre,
book columnist for *The Phoenix* and *Steps For Recovery*